RIZZOLI
NEW YORK

New York Paris London Milan

IF POETRY IS ABOUT LOVE
AND ART IS ABOUT LOVE
AND MUSIC IS ABOUT LOVE
AND THEATRE IS ABOUT LOVE
AND IF OPERA IS ABOUT LOVE...
WHY DO WE THINK DESIGN
IS ABOUT FUNCTIONALITY?

I dedicate this book to Karin, without her nothing in this book would have been realized

Staging Spaces

by Robert Thiemann

Exactly ten years ago I interviewed Marcel Wanders for *Frame*. While rereading the article, it struck me how much has stayed the same in the professional life of Wanders. Take for example his view on the profession of the designer. "I see design as a way to tell a story," he told me back then. "For me, designing revolves around the fact that what I make means something to other people, around the notion that design communicates," he continued. He still holds this opinion today. He also stated ten years ago that the profession of the designer had to be redefined by injecting it with the qualities behind love and amateurism. Herewith he referred to passion, frankness, and the need to experiment—all qualities that professionals eventually tend to lose throughout the course of their career. He continues to hold this view today as well.

Meanwhile, a lot has changed for the designer Marcel Wanders. While he was mainly designing products in 2000, he has now expanded his scope to interiors, architecture, and even project planning. This gives him the opportunity to place his products within their dreamed context. The last ten years, the amateur inside of him has developed as well. When one tries to remember his first big interior project—the VIP lounge of the Dutch pavilion at the Expo 2000 in Hannover—one visualizes a design based on a single idea: the creation of a continuously changing light by means of hundreds of roughly shaped, silver-colored objects hanging from the ceiling. An enthralling, yet simple concept. Here, he still behaved like a product designer, basing every object on one strong idea. Of similar simplicity is his Mandarina Duck store in London. It was only because of breathing, human-like figures and a singular giant that the straightforward design of the space escaped the sense of "professionalism" that it was meant to convey.

Wanders' breakthrough as an interior designer followed in 2005, when he designed the Lute Suites in Amsterdam in cooperation with senior designer Karin Krautgartner. Seven apartments were furnished with numerous designs of their own. This project differed from the rest of his early work because Wanders dared to deal with the complete space. No single surface was left blank: the designers' signatures were visible from the floor to the ceiling. "Our clients ask us for who we are. And that is exactly what we present to them: us," explains Wanders.

While the Lute Suites are not the most compelling of Wanders' work, they functioned as the big leap towards the visually overwhelming environments that Wanders and his team designed between 2008 and 2010: the Mondrian South Beach hotel in Miami, the fashion store Villa Moda in Bahrain and the Kameha Grand in Bonn. In these commercial projects, the creative energy is endless. Floors and walls exhibit floral patterns. Doors and columns—adorned with intricate reliefs—gain added depth and conjure up an image of oversized chessmen. Surreal pictures of young women enhance the few empty spaces. Intense scaling and Baroque decorations are elements that recur throughout the space, just like the colors black, white and red—flanked by accents of silver and gold. As a finishing touch, an abstract image of Wanders' head pops up at unexpected places, interchanged at times with another beloved symbol: the gold nose of a clown.

Wanders' interiors project a fairytale-like romanticism. Each one, in every conceivable way, is flamboyant, rich in detail and larger than life. They communicate the notion of luxury in a direct and frank way. Here, more is more. One cannot escape this world, but is washed over by it.

And this is exactly what Wanders' has in mind. "Others deliver an interior design," he says. "But we offer a reason for a visit, we create a destination." In his interiors, visitors need to feel special, more beautiful, better. In the meantime, his designs need to be understandable and direct. They cannot put up any possible

Although originally educated as a chemical engineer, Robert Thiemann became a copywriter and developed into a prolific journalist. His writing specializes in design, with a strong focus on interiors. In 1997 he co-founded FRAME: THE GREAT INDOORS, an international bi-monthly magazine devoted to contemporary interior and product design, of which he still is Editor in Chief. Currently distributed in over fifty-two countries, FRAME is considered an authoritative resource in the world of design. Thiemann is also shareholder of Frame Publishers, which launched its first book in 2001 with a monograph on the work of Fabio Novembre, and continues to publish books that cover subjects as diverse as the design of trade-fair stands and the in-depth exploration of building on water. In 2005, he co-founded MARK: ANOTHER ARCHITECTURE, a bimonthly international trade journal featuring exceptional architecture projects around the world, of which he's also Editor in Chief.

♦

barrier. It is because of this that Wanders' designs are loaded with symbols that are easily identifiable—symbols that one can relate to without much effort. Flowers, hearts, the color red; one can call them clichés, even kitsch, but no one can possibly deny their central theme: love. One of Wanders' merits is that he is able to take these clichés to another level—a level way beyond the ordinary, where they can provide a special experience. This makes Wanders more of a "people's designer" than a "designer's designer"—he designs for the user instead of his colleagues.

Wanders does not work in a vacuum. He attributes his main influence to Starck, whom he sees as being the best designer in the world. Their affinity is particularly visible in their hotel designs. It is not a coincidence that both designers had their breakthrough at the Morgans Hotel Group: Starck with the Royalton, Paramount and Delano, and Wanders with the Mondrian South Beach Hotel. Both designers are in turn influenced by the groundbreaking work of Andrée Putman for the Morgans hotel, an establishment that is part of the same hotel chain and is regarded as one of the first "boutique hotels." What is already visible in the work of Putman—the role of the designer as a film director—is amplified by Starck and Wanders. Both think in sequences of images, not in separate stills. Their story starts even before one enters the hotel: on the driveway. Entrance, lobby, restaurant, corridors—all are designed in coherence, like elements of the same story. Their interiors are more like theater designs than neutral containers, and Starck and Wanders are the directors—arranging their pieces and creating the preconditions for a show in their consciously staged spaces. Anyone looking for clues about Wanders' future interior designs need only look at these staged spaces. As a designer, Wanders realizes more and more that interior design offers him the possibility to use time as a tool he can play with—a possibility that product design lacks. He is not only able to assemble the

past, present and future by connecting clichés and technological inventions, but is also capable of designing interiors in which different experiences flow consecutively in time. In the words of Wanders himself: "One can listen to a CD, but one could also visit an opera and even sit on the stage of the opera, which will cause the level of experience to increase. This is the challenge of interior design: to create complex environments, in order to stimulate an audience to derive as much as possible from the experience."

I will not be surprised when he succeeds.

The Outside-the-Box Interior Life of Marcel Wanders

by Linda Tischler

No one would ever accuse Marcel Wanders of being emotionally inhibited. His interiors, in all their puckish, often surreal glory, are the work of a man who's unafraid of bucking trends, who's unapologetically exuberant, and who's comfortable enough in his own skin to sign his work with an image of himself sporting a gold clown's nose.

For Wanders, the modern design mantra of "less is more" feels, well, a tad stingy. Who would want to live in a space, he argues, where the designer was inspired to do *less* than he could? The very idea is inconceivable. Instead, he sees the spaces he creates as gifts to their inhabitants, as precious and personal as if they were tied with ribbons and accompanied by cake and candles. As a child in Holland, Wanders pondered what qualities went into a great present. Imagine, he thought, if you opened the box, and discovered something that perfectly suited you—but that you didn't even realize you needed. Not only would that be a good gift, but it would make you feel deeply understood by the giver. Even better would be a gift that also showed the hand of its creator.

Wanders' environments inspire that kind of wonder and delight; to experience them is to inhabit a space unlike any other. I remember the first time I stayed at the Wanders-designed Mondrian Hotel in South Beach. The hotel had just opened, and the city's cabbies had yet to discover it. As my taxi pulled into the *porte-cochere*, under its magnificent gold bell-shaped chandeliers, the driver let out a low whistle. "Holy smoke," he said (OK, his language was a bit earthier than that). "Look at that!" Need I mention that Miami taxi drivers are not easily surprised? The magic continued as I walked over the threshold, entering a dreamscape filled with Jack-and-the-Beanstalk-sized columns, white lollipop-shaped trees, and a lacy black staircase that curved up into the clouds.

But the best was yet to come. The pool deck, in many hotels an expanse of chairs with all the charm of a bus station waiting room, was instead, a surreal tableau that was cinematically beautiful. Red baroque chairs, love seats and cushions, were arrayed on a red and white patterned carpet. Sky-high sheer, billowing draperies framed a spectacular view of Miami's skyline. Ivy-covered arches, sheltering secret sofas, provided discreet settings for amorous lovers. It was all so spellbinding, it took my breath away. I knew in a flash that this was a place for mystery and magic, not just lodging and dining. "I want to include fantasy in my work," Wanders says, noting that the surreal and fantastic are concepts more often appended to works in the theatre or film than to interior design. "We can do beautiful things, but we'd rather go one step further, creating something strange or surprising."

A business hotel is the last place you'd expect to find either the strange or the surprising. But at the Kameha Grand Bonn, Wanders broke from the convention dictating that hotels catering to corporate clients need to look like the lodging equivalent of gray flannel suits. Instead, the Kameha takes guests on a psychedelic trip through another dimension where pharaoh-sized urns double as columns, chandeliers look like they've escaped from a giant's Christmas tree, and a full, glowing moon rises over a headboard. One couple told a travel website that they loved the place because they never knew what they'd find around a corner. Precisely. If this hotel doesn't jumpstart creative thinking, then business groups should be forced to stay home and do trust falls in the company cafeteria.

That same penchant for surprising visitors is amply on display at Wanders' souk-inspired shop for Villa Moda in Bahrain. The store, which rotates its merchandise every few days, extends its extreme devotion to the unpredictable in its décor. There are stairs that lead to nowhere. Doors that don't open. Corners that

Linda Tischler is a senior writer at FAST COMPANY, *where she has become known for her extensive coverage on the intersection of business and design. For the past several years, she has been responsible for the magazine's inspiring October "Masters of Design" issue, which celebrates people in the forefront of design thinking. Tischler also oversees the design coverage and blogs for Fastcompany.com, and played a crucial role in launching the site's team of expert design bloggers. She has addressed and moderated several design events and forums around the world, including ones for the Association of Professional Design Firms and AIGA, the professional association for design.*

◆

don't really match up. It's Wanders whimsy at full throttle. The color scheme is black and white, to throw the rich tones of the wares into bold relief.

Wanders began his career in product design creating, among other things, the fanciful Knotted Chair, a feat of technological wizardry that made an ethereal construction of macramé rope into a chair capable of supporting a body. He went on to mastermind other products that melded design virtuosity with mesmerizing creativity—a chandelier for Flos that hid lavish architectural detailing under a severe black shade, a pillowy chair that a Dutch granny might have crocheted, and a vase modeled on airborne snot.

Murray Moss, the famed curator of the New York design emporium, Moss, says Wanders has an extraordinary ability to meld technological innovation with the humanistic qualities of craft. "Marcel's work often has you saying, 'Why have I never seen this before?'—and then you realize it's because it didn't exist before," Moss says. "It looks so familiar, and so friendly. It's because he's comfortable with new technology, but doesn't work with it in a way that flags it as 'techno.'" It was only after Wanders mastered the demands of product design that he felt ready for the challenge of interiors. Space, he says, has a raft of needs that products don't. It needs to flow around you, to tell you different things at different times of day. "In product design, I am a sculptor, working in marble," he says. "In interiors, I feel like a composer, creating an opera." Wanders is now a global brand, recognized from Dubai to L.A. But lately, his work has increasingly referenced his Dutch background. It's both an homage to his wildly creative homeland, and another signal to his audience that the work you see before you has a pedigree, a heritage, a cultural connection. He has written a book about the creative history of Amsterdam, and developed a site, Westerhuis, that houses 50,000 square feet of space for creative industries in

the city. "Amsterdam has become more in my eyes and my heart these days, " he says. This project, among others, has made him a hero in his hometown. "Marcel is an icon of the creative industry, and an inspiring role model for young designers, " says Carolien Gehrels, Deputy Mayor of Amsterdam. While Westerhuis is one of his newest projects, it's far from the first to tap his interest in historic preservation. Early on, Wanders recognized that the rich cultural history of the region presented unique opportunities for exploring the thrilling intersection of the old and the new.

That Dutch design DNA is increasingly finding a place in his most modern incarnations. A condo in Miami has Delft tile on the kitchen's backsplash, a sleek modern house in Mallorca is outfitted with a classically proportioned breakfront, the stools in a hip bar in New York sport spindled backs, as if they were plucked from a tavern in Leiden. It's a way of reminding people to respect the old, not just in a mischievous game of, "Name that provenance," but as a way of teaching us a primary principle of sustainability: that the most enduring objects are those that we cherish enough to keep for a long time, not replace instantly when something newer comes along. "I've lately been pushing references to history, to give more life to my projects," Wanders says. "I'd like to change the opinion of design to be modern only. Respect for our past plays a different role than sixty years ago. It's my contribution to the sustainability conversation." Modern and antique. Sober and fanciful. Elegant and whimsical. Fearless and sentimental. Sexy, sustainable, and snotty. Marcel Wanders is a welter of contradictions that make him truly one of a kind. What is the source of this extraordinary artistry? Seemingly, some inexhaustible wellspring of creativity deep inside. "Tie me to a chair, blindfold me," he says. "I'll be fine. Inspiration comes from within, there is an endless source, ideas are always coming."

Casa Son Vida

"ROOTS ARE ATTACHED TO TRADITION, BUT TREES ARE DIRECTIONS TO THE FUTURE"

The first full residential project of Marcel Wanders, the 850-square meter residence embodies Marcels' vision in each of its curved corners. The conversion and extension of the Mediterranean, Sixties-era villa gave birth to a friendly meeting between old and new. The subtle mix of classical and modern references is visible throughout the entire villa—from the classic, profiled wall lining the curved space, to the new, custom designed cupboards in straight, elegant lines. A unique atmosphere emerges as the space turns into a playground for reliefs and surfaces. A house of contrasts that displays a love for past and present, Casa Son Vida is "unavoidably exuberant and unabashedly outrageous".

marcel wanders · casa son vida · 2008

"Roots are attached to tradition,
but trees are directions
to the future"

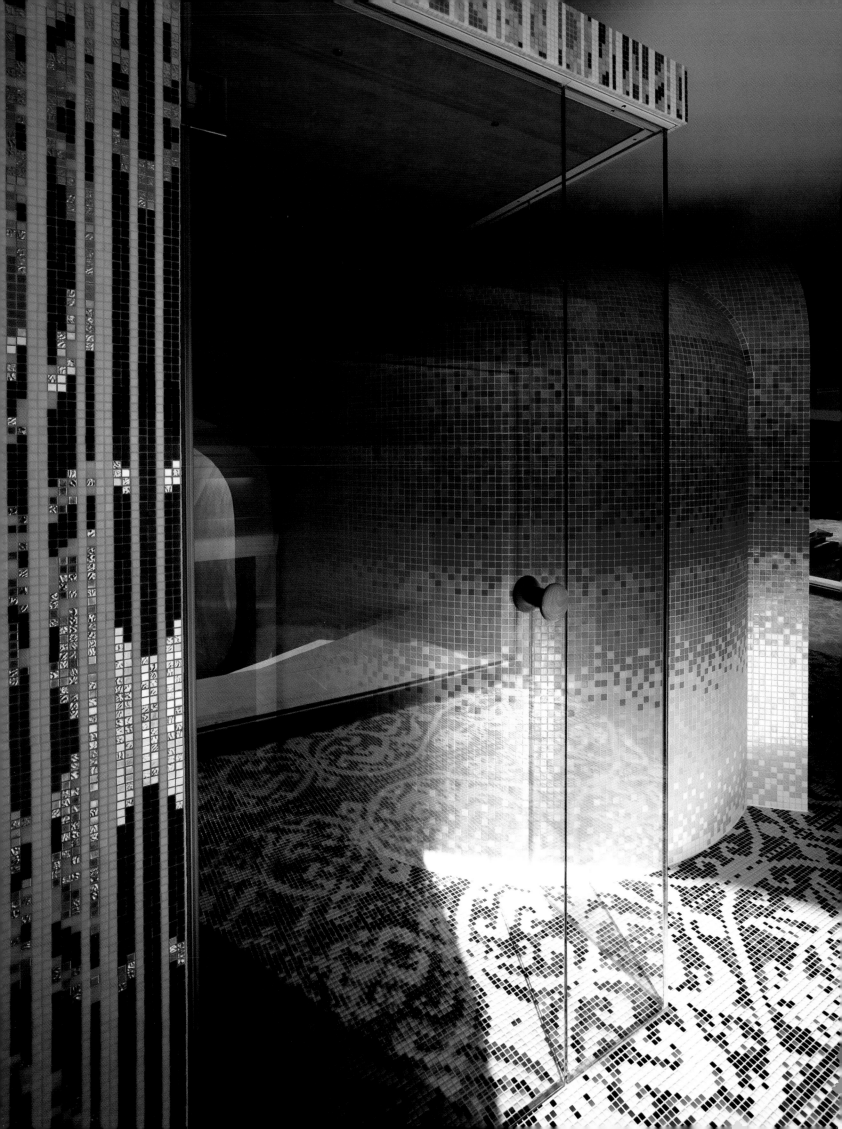

Daydreams

PROJECT: *Dome Of Dreams*

INTENTION: *Practicing to believe the impossible*

DETAIL: *Mermaid Pool*

LOCATION: *Abu Dhabi*

TIME: *16.04*

EMOTION: *Hopeful*

HOPE: *Vision with*

Villa Amsterdam

PRIVATE RESIDENCE — 2008

◆

"IF YOU THINK SKIN IS SURFACE AND SURFACE IS
SUPERFICIAL, YOUR BRAIN HAS PROVEN THAT YOUR
EYES DON'T WORK"

With 102 square meters of space and a garden that is 100 square meters, Villa Amsterdam strangely symbolizes the typical residence in the Netherlands. With these specifications, the space had to be very rationally organized. But rationality doesn't stop architecture from speaking. The interior of Villa Amsterdam abounds with strong details that impart a sense of monumentality. The semi-circular wall in the main area was enhanced and the curved wall bulged to give an iconic presence to the space. The boundary between inside and outside, and between architecture and nature are blurred. The garden and the house had to live together in a beautiful, peaceful way.

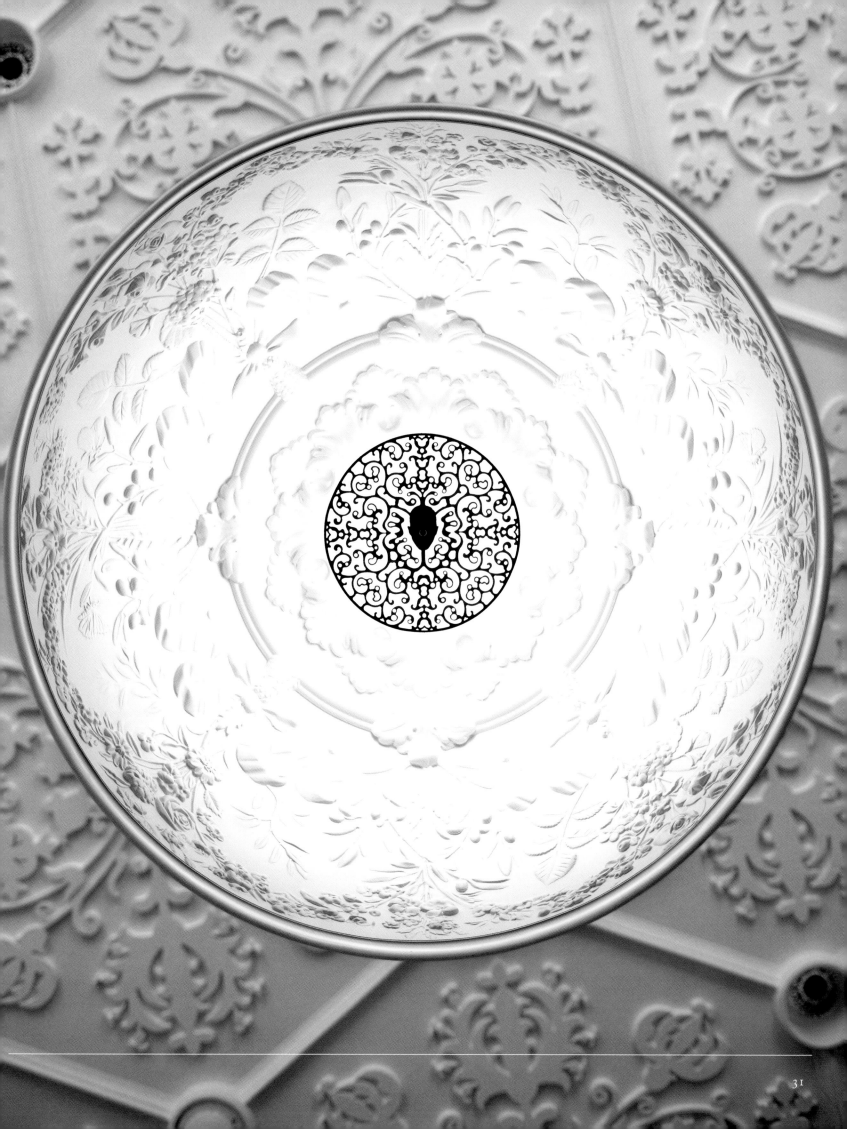

"If you think skin is surface and surface is superficial, your brain has proven that your eyes don't work"

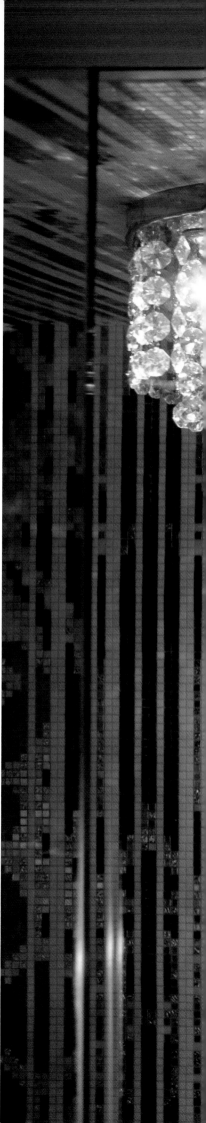

Time & Space

TIME & SPACE — Time is the crucial element, the most important link in the chain. It contains gifts from the past and measures our contribution to the future. Time sets the stage for our temporary theater. A theater of joy, surprise, recognition and wonder. It allows me to tell a story, to take you on a journey, from a minute-long tale to stories the length of an opera. Time walks you through space, experiencing the flavors of the day, the uniqueness of each ray of sunlight and the presence of others. It is time which allows us to see all these different aspects of space and which makes us understand the order and organization of it. Space is a shelter, is a void, is a womb. It is welcoming—for us to be in, go through, to enjoy. Architecture is hard and rigid as human bodies are soft and fragile. Walk naked in a naked building and you will feel violence. So we dress both, hoping they can coexist together. Interiors are essential to architecture as clothes are to people. Space gives depth to our vision and puts on show the power we represent. Space can thrive on contrasts, but I love the internal connections, the minute similarities, a family tree of connections, legible at first glance. The blurring, of inside and outside, the little lies we create. I don't like formality, I'd rather be touched, moved. I love the connections space can make with its context, its history. The ultimate dream is still to create space beyond time, a space that will live forever, a space that will grow graceful with age. In a time where the realities of context and function are so volatile, eternity is a hard, perhaps even impossible task. And so we find that the ultimate destination of space is to live in the hearts of people, to go on a journey for a lifetime, in a strangers heart.

Marcel Wanders

MIAMI SOUTH BEACH, BOUTIQUE HOTEL – 2008

◆

"AFTER A HUNDRED YEARS OF SLEEP ONE SEES THE WORLD WITH FRESH NEW EYES"

Also known as Sleeping Beauty's castle, The Mondrian South Beach (Morgans Hotel Group) at Biscayne Bay in Miami Beach is a true modern fantasy. Chic and dramatic living spaces are furnished with original, bespoke pieces that include iconic items such as carved chairs, milled tables, vine cabanas and a signature floating staircase. The mirrored, mosaic spa-reception desk scatters light across the dimly lit room. Black and gold patterned furnishings, oversized, brass, bell-shaped lights, kissing corners in the garden, private party places and an aqua spa add a magical touch to the hotel's atmosphere. The Mondrian South Beach's wonderful world has no limits, with four South Beach Sky Terrace Suites with butler service, a fitness area open 24 hours a day, a business facility centre and the Mondrian Marina's stunning views of the Atlantic Ocean, Biscayne Bay and downtown Miami. Surrounding the hotel are oases of lush gardens, an outdoor pool, bars and private cabanas with curtains of living foliage. The walls of the hotel's restaurant, Asia de Cuba, are paneled with mirrors, catching the last sunrays of the day through wide windows and scattering them across the room. As a tribute to this gorgeous, filtered light, the bar opposite from the restaurant is named the "Sunset Lounge." Welcome to a Wanders Wonderland: a fantastic environment where sophistication and exotic, fine tastes find their roots.

The Mondrian South Beach Hotel became winner of the International Hotel/Motel/Restaurant Show's Gold Key Award in 2009 for Best Lounge/Bar. The same year, the Mondrian South Beach Hotel was nominated for the Great Indoors Award in the Relax & Consume Category.

"After a hundred years of sleep one sees the world with fresh new eyes"

Daydreams

PROJECT: *Dome Of Dreams*

INTENTION: *Feel the skin feed the inside*

DETAIL: *Summer Shower*

LOCATION: *Abu Dhabi*

TIME: *15.28*

EMOTION: *Glow*

HOPE: *Eternity*

THOR, NEW YORK, RESTAURANT — 2004

Located in one of Manhattan's most diverse and creative neighborhoods, the Lower East Side, the Hotel on Rivington flourishes as a hotspot by perfectly capturing the style and the individuality of that area. The hotel's grand entrance, lobby, bar, private bar and full-service restaurant, Thor, offer an impressive experience. The airy dining room features an 8-meter, soaring glass ceiling with views of the Lower East Side's historic tenement buildings. The cutting-edge design flaunts a Swarovski crystal-embedded bar, white pebbled walls, and water-tables with high-tech animals that create the lighting effects of the bar. The interior of the Hotel on Rivington is a celebration of the artistic energy of downtown Manhattan.

EXT.
DOOR

Daydreams

PROJECT: *Monastry of Bookless Wisdom*

INTENTION: *I dream of creating green clouds*

DETAIL: *View of the wisdom treasure building*

LOCATION: *Strait of Malacca*

TIME: *07.13*

EMOTION: *Universal connection*

HOPE: *Insight*

Haryadi Residence

PRIVATE RESIDENCE — 2008

◆

"TO DESIGN A HOUSE FOR A FRIEND IS EVEN MORE DIFFICULT THAN DESIGNING ONE'S OWN HOUSE"

A three-story miracle house, designed for a hidden place in the Jakarta jungle, this residence was also designed as a concrete jewel box: keeping the world outside while keeping the beauty inside. Using sun and wind as his friends, the house is able to live on natural air-conditioning. Sun-facing walls are closed, while wind-facing walls can use their transparency to support a cool flow of fresh air.

To design a house for a friend is even more difficult than designing one's own house. You visit, enjoy the place and go home afterwards leaving your friends with all your mistakes. I hope once the mistakes are found, they will be forgiven.

"To design a house for a friend is even more difficult than designing one's own house"

Daydreams

PROJECT: *Monastry of Bookless Wisdom*

INTENTION: *Where wise men speak wise men are silent*

DETAIL: *Table for silver words*

LOCATION: *Strait of Malacca*

TIME: *13.48*

EMOTION: *Generous compassion*

HOPE: *Understanding*

AMSTERDAM BOUTIQUE HOTEL – 2005

◆

"BUILT IN THE YEAR THAT BACH COMPOSED THE LUTE SUITES, AND FINALLY FINISHED FOR US TO ENJOY THE MUSIC"

Lute Suites was born from an innovative and unparalleled concept conceived by Pete Lute and Marcel Wanders. The interior of each of the 7 suites and 3 boardrooms is utterly unique in every detail, fitted out with every imaginable comfort. Converted from exquisitely beautiful, 18th century cottages with all-commanding views of the Amstel river and the spectacular Dutch skies, the Lute Suites offer complete freedom of movement to their guests. Simultaneously modern and classical, the suites combine global style with a warm, welcoming ambiance. All the suites have their own front door and are comprised of a living room, a separate bedroom, a bathroom, and a kitchenette.

In 2005 Marcel Wanders received an award nomination for the Lensvelt Architect Interior Prize for Lute Suites.

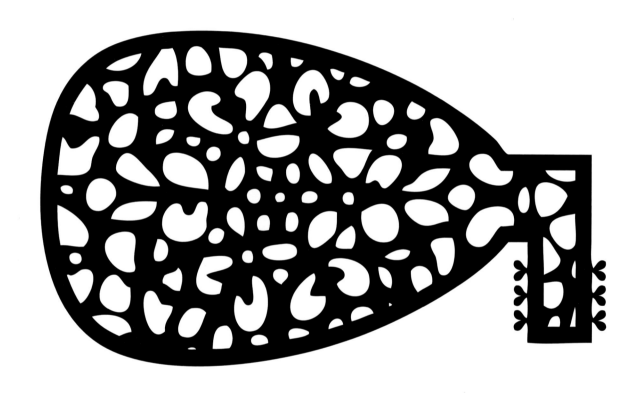

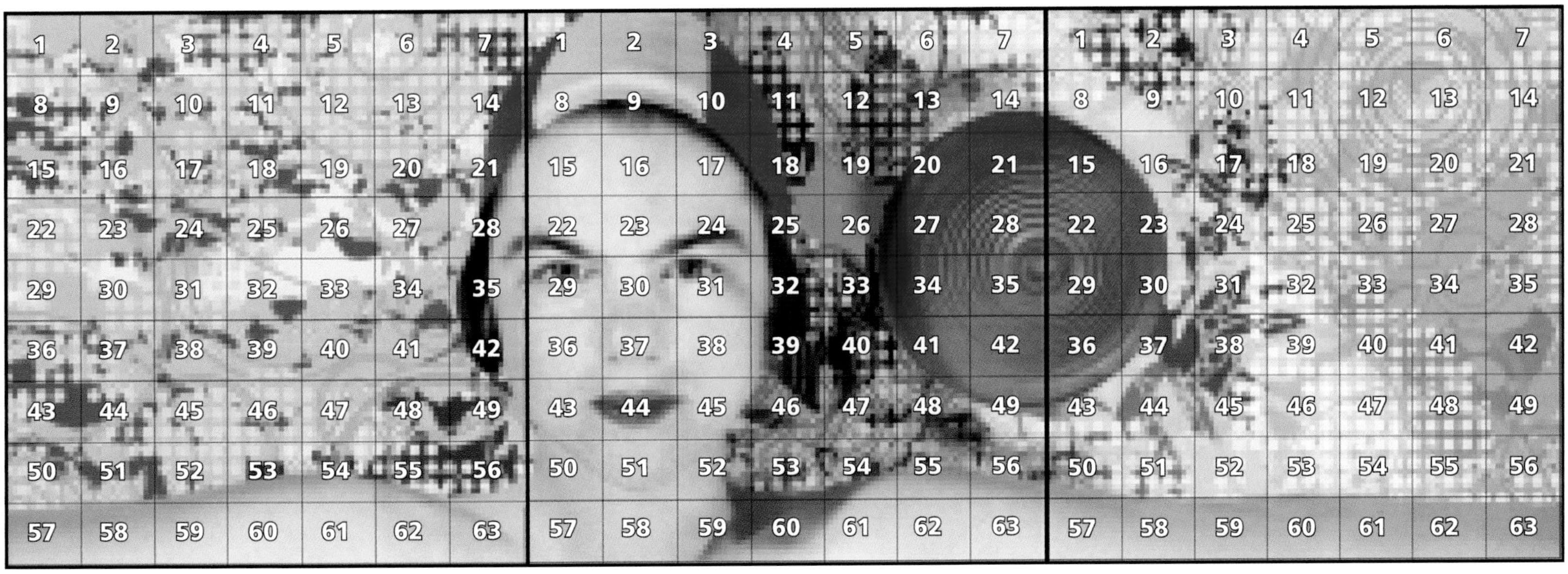

"Built in the year that Bach composed the Lute Suites, and finally finished for us to enjoy the music"

ME — Call me if you need me! I will be your guide, your medium to the surreal. I will dream you dreams you've never dreamt. Two stilts keep me up: one is called brain, the other, heart. I never walk. I run or I dance. I spin between polarities, hardly touching middle ground. There is no terrain unfit for my humanist-freedom-dance. There are no rules, no scripts, no dogmas, no borders—sullen fundamentalists can watch impotently and grumpily from a corner of the room. In my dance, fantasy rules. In my dance, I celebrate time and space. There is no need for revolution because its brutal force will keep us from dance. We are parents of the evolution, the eternal dance of life. This dance creates families, creates histories, creates romance. Permit me to describe my passion, to show you my love. This is my ultimate goal, to share the impossible, to supercede expectations, and after that, to give even more. Design is an international language, it transcends the limits of time and culture, it celebrates the fruits of culture and it connects. Me... I am my family. Me... I am the link to others. Me... A universe of uncles and sisters guide me on my path. Me... I am my studio... a thousand brilliant minds. I play Santa. I hope they love my gifts.

Marcel Wanders

Heart of Europe

MASTERPLAN FOR DUBAI ISLAND GROUP — 2009

"IF YOU WANT AMSTERDAM, YOU STILL HAVE TO COME TO AMSTERDAM"

On the coast of Dubai, in the bright blue waters, there was a plan. Islands—shaping the world map, country by country—were created from soil. Visionary, silly, fabulous, magic, daring… we were asked to create the Netherlands, equipped with an art center for artists in residence, an exhibition hall, galleries and an outdoor theatre on top of it all. Imagine an elliptical, 5-star hotel with a central garden, rooftop swimming pool and access to a red light discotheque. Or windmills with apartments on a pitch and putting green, overlooking 3 towers with hovering, helium-filled moons. Or shopping all around, with cool beach clubs and marinas, floating private-party islands, floating pools and floating solar-islands. And so many more ideas, down the drain, into the ocean. This won't be built: they didn't plan on making coffee shops and red light windows. If you want Amsterdam, you still have to come to Amsterdam.

"If you want Amsterdam, you still have to come to Amsterdam"

Daydreams

PROJECT: *Monastry of Bookless Wisdom*

INTENTION: *Connecting knowledge with vision*

DETAIL: *Garden of introspection*

LOCATION: *Strait of Malacca*

TIME: *08.34*

EMOTION: *Discombobulated*

HOPE: *All is one, one is all*

BAHRAIN PILOT STORE — 2009

"VILLA MODA BAHRAIN IS THE
INTERNATIONAL SOUK"

The *souk* is the ultimate marketplace: a concentration of innovation and tradition, diversity and intimacy. It pulses with the richness of overlapping cultures that results as goods and people come together. Completed in 2008, Villa Moda showcases the rich artisanship of local craftsmen, motifs and techniques, re-interpreted with Western eyes. Theses local crafts were used to compose a complex textured scheme, adding depth to an otherwise modest black and white color palette, and leaving color for the guests. The 1,050-square meter store in Bahrain is laid out like a small city, with each building housing a specific department or brand. As clients shop within this "International Souk," they are treated to a bevy of innovative luxury brands.

Villa Moda was nominated in 2009 for the Condé Nast Traveller Innovation and Design Awards for Interior Design in the Retail category.

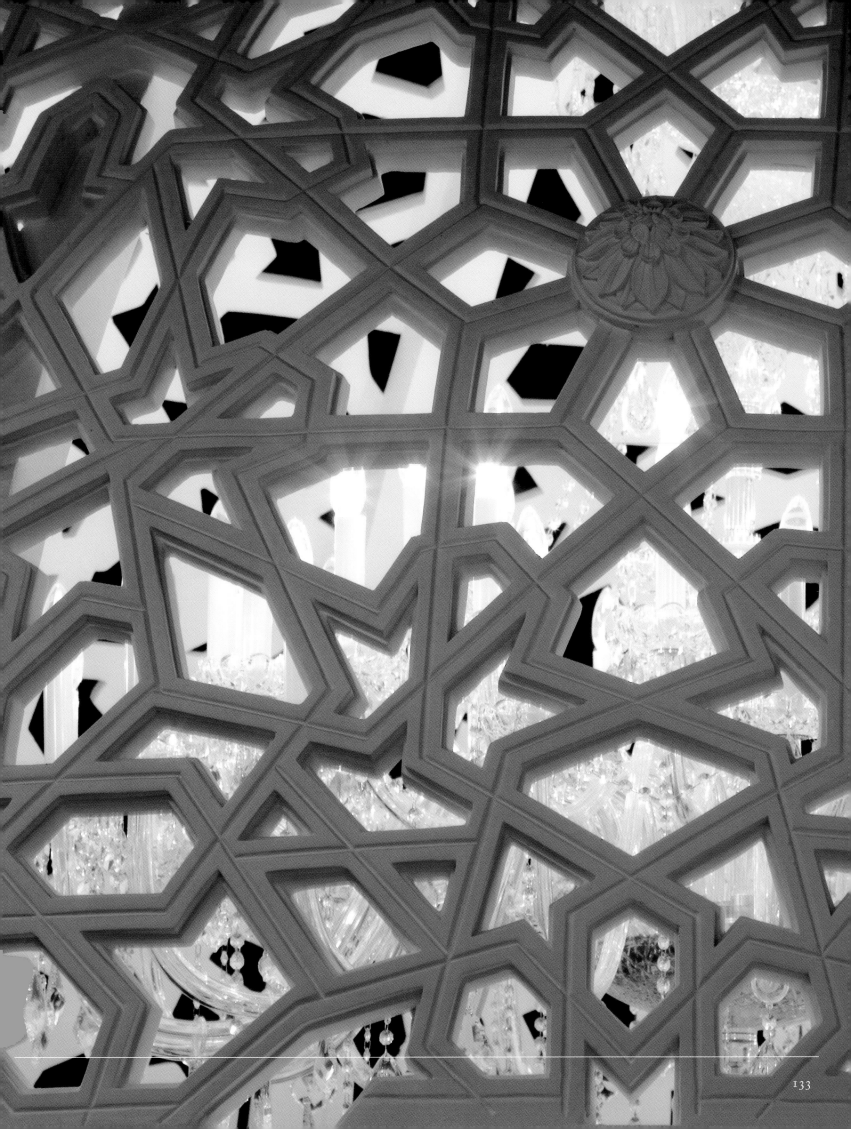

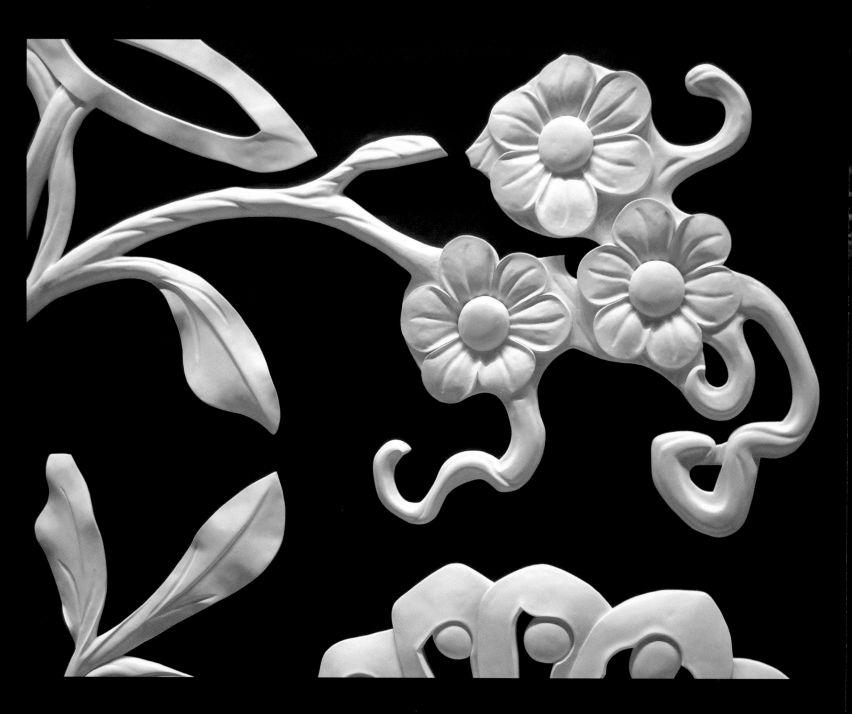

"*Villa Moda Bahrain is the international souk*"

You

YOU — Standing by the door, waiting for your next day, for your next step. With the ultimate belief that tomorrow will be wonderful. Let me be your host for today. Let me invite you to my world, which exists in your world. May I share the pleasure of creation, may I show the happiness of people, and for your perusal, my insane vanity. And please understand it as a mirror, a reflection of my true self. You are invited to this tournament of beauty, with daffodils and lilies, in chocolate and magenta, triangles of gold, peopled by faeries, beauties and beasts. All play a role in this timely cabaret. May I direct this theatre? Be for once the composer of your day, the jester and your friend? I will give you all I have and hold little back. For what is in the heart will stay in the heart and what is not made with it can never enter. So may I ask you, dear guest, to open your eyes and enjoy the ride? Remember these pleasures as a child, and this ride is yours for now and forever. A critical spirit will show you what you will forget—but wide open eyes will show you what you will always remember.

Marcel Wanders

LONDON PILOT STORE — 2002

"THE REMAINING QUESTION WILL ALWAYS BE, 'HOW DO YOU SEIZE THE WILLY OF A 7-METER TALL, YELLOW GULLIVER?'"

Mandarina Duck is an Italian brand known mainly for its luggage. With this UK concept store, Mandarina Duck wanted to introduce its fashion line to the public. We called the store the house of Gulliver—the legendary British traveler. Gulliver, with a built-in speaker-system and his full, bright yellow posture, stands 7 meters tall in the store and his presence connects the two floors of the building. Around him, clothing and bags are presented on glass tables and shelves and come to life on 40 subtle breathing mannequins. With this subtle movement, they bring the brand and the building to life. In the same way, a large, two-story high, chromed, mirrored wall also breathes life into the space as it changes its surface from convex to concave in a constant fluid rhythm. The store's front window presents the Wanders one word-weekly-magazine. Outside, there is a constant stream of air-bubbles floating around the building and small foam heaps that visualize the living identity of the brand, the building and the city of London.

*"The remaining question
will always be, 'how do you seize
the willy of a 7-meter tall, yellow
Gulliver?'"*

Expo 2000

◆

Designed especially for the Hanover World Exposition 2000, the Royal Wing Room was conceived as the heart of the green island floating on the top of the Dutch pavilion designed by MVRDV architects. The space brought an otherworldly feeling to its visitors. The tour started with the discovery of a big, oval, white floor with curled up borders that resemble an empty ice rink waiting for skaters. The shiny, snow-white floor reflects the highlights of thousands of silver twigs, spread across the curved ceiling. A cunning lighting system was set-up to create the sensation of an artificial skylight; without any windows in the room, it still appeared as though the rays of the sun were gleaming into the room, followed by the shadows of invisible clouds. During this light experience, the air was filled with the crystalline sound of clinking wine glasses that were mounted discreetly between the silvery twigs on the sparkling ceiling. Even the specially woven tablecloth seemed to mirror the glittery objects above. The inhabitants of the Royal Wing Room were the VIP chairs, all of which were a unique color and equipped with hidden wheels that transformed every evening into a dinner dance.

Daydreams

PROJECT: *The endless opera of sun + moon connection*

<u>INTENTION</u>: *Understanding the harmony of polarity*

<u>DETAIL</u>: *Crystal Hall*

#6/7

<u>LOCATION</u>: *Moskva*

<u>TIME</u>: *Relatively unknown*

<u>EMOTION</u>: *Quietly excited*

<u>HOPE</u>: *Universal*

"ONE SPEAKS OF IT IN AMSTERDAM!"

Rotter-*damned* potent, and Amster-*damned* charming, a restaurant like a theatre. As evening falls, it's time for the audience to take the stage. The spectators and theater merge into one; who is the audience, who are the actors? No one knows. The Rotterdam audience is the star of the evening; bottles are poured with charisma and bravado, and all around bread and fish are miraculously multiplied. The stage is scattered with props, and the formalities of the performance make way for chance encounters and unwritten romance. Young couples, avoiding the gaze of the crowd, line up at the blind date suite, where they can safely drown in one another's eyes. With the day's work done, it's party time—with rolled up sleeves or formal attire, barefoot or high heeled. Laughter fills the room, and the sorrow of the day makes way for the sensuality of night. The tired players peer into the darkened hall, the floodlit ships float past on the murmuring stream, the water whispers, and under the glistening moon the actors' costumes get critiqued. Heavenly gold fills the lower, waterside stage. Here, not all that glitters is gold. Tomorrow is another day. The waters will flow; the Maas river is no longer alone.

"Young couples, avoiding the gaze of the crowd, line up at the blind date suite, where they can safely drown in one another's eyes"

"One speaks of it in Amsterdam!"

JVC Building

DESIGN FOR A GUADALAJARA APARTMENT BUILDING — 2004

◆

"I DREAM OF CREATING GREEN CLOUDS"

I dream of creating a functional living environment which enriches human life and supports and inspires personal as well as world ecology. I dream of creating a soft, human building—supporting the individuality and health of people and making spaces for their dreams, passions and personal growth. I dream of creating an innovative, eco-logical building—learning from nature and technology to inspire architecture as well as the general public. I dream of creating an open fortress which makes the inhabitants feel safe and protected and is a welcome, new garden for a city of flowers.

I dream of creating green clouds.

Winner of the competition for Omnilife, 2003

Against
design
fundamentalism

THE CONTEMPORARY RENAISSANCE OF HUMANISM — Fundamentalism. You strictly believe and adhere to a set of basic principles. Principles that limit your freedom. You impose these principles on others, so they cannot enjoy the freedom you are lacking. Anyone who does not comply with the same principles as you do—independent of their own principles and beliefs—is a sinner.

Within the world of design there is a severe and almost religious belief in the old dogmas. And we are taught to protect these dogmas, or the personal interpretation of dogmas that we call our own opinion, with force. The world is becoming bigger every day; increasingly more people cross our path with different cultures, beliefs and ideas. Communication on a large scale is possible, making this big world the perfect setting to learn from each other. Instead, we are all constrained by the same old principles and dogmas. Worse, we claim the rules and impose them on others. We have created a world in which good design is virtually universally identical and at the same time controlled within our personal monopoly.

I have nothing against the old dogmas of design, they have survived the test of time and brought us where we are today. But I think the world has so much more to offer, and we have so much more to offer to the world. In nature it is always variety that is the most crucial factor for success. We are fundamentalists in our design mentality: we are blind and we defend our blind eyes with so much force and certainty that we are unable to see it. Viewed from a distance, we would be shamefully amused by the imaginative certainty we think we have.

Why do we think that other designers should follow our rules in design?

Why is it so different to try to understand their point of view and learn instead of teach?

Let's be designers of the future.

Let's forget our cynical, negative approach to the unknown, and instead embrace it.

Let's trust the positive intentions of our colleagues.

This is all we need to do to act against design fundamentalism!

Marcel Wanders

AMSTERDAM, MULTITENANT CULTURAL FLAGSHIP BUILDING — 2008

"WHO NEEDS A NEST MORE, THE CHICKEN OR THE EGG??"

With a surface area of 5,500 square meters, Westerhuis is devoted to the creative industry of Amsterdam and has grown into a cultural platform. The majority of the spaces have been leased to a mixture of art and design studios, architects and art galleries amongst others. In addition, part of the building hosts the studio of Marcel Wanders, Moooi gallery and an international exhibition place. As a unique, top-level center for art and culture, the Westerhuis is an important hub for the creative industry in Amsterdam.

Westerhuis is realized in partnership with Aedes Real Estate.

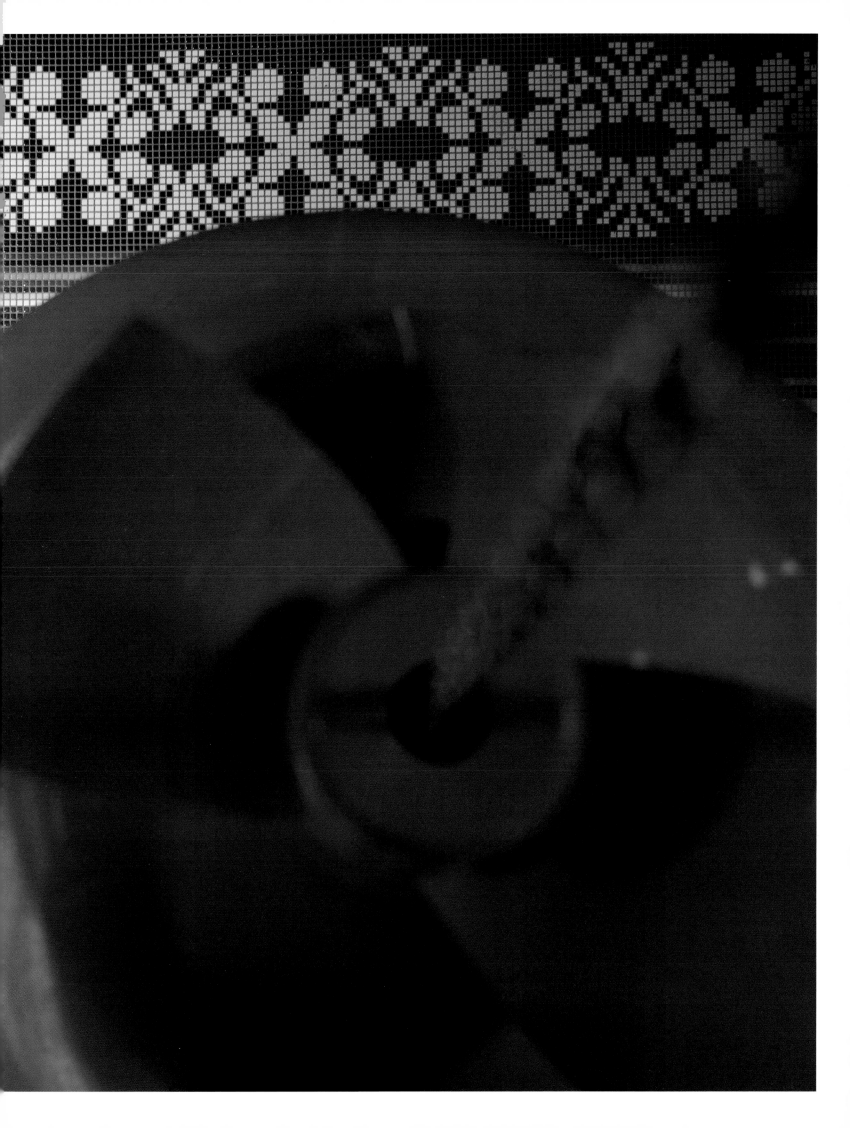

"Who needs a nest more, the chicken or the egg?"

Daydreams

PROJECT: *The endless opera of sun +*
moon connection

INTENTION: *Materializing virtual wisdom*

DETAIL: *Miniature model of the wisdom treasure*
building

LOCATION: *Moskva*

TIME: *Relative*

EMOTION: *Peaceful in*
absence of knowledge

HOPE: *Visualization of*
trust

Stonehouse

TILBURG, INTERPOLIS HEADQUATERS — 2002

"WHO NEEDS A WELL-LIT DESK IF HE CAN CHOOSE TO WORK IN THE PARK?"

The Interpolis Stonehouse is part of the main office for the insurance company Interpolis located in Tilburg, the Netherlands. The whole staff works at flexible workstations. For these 3,000 employees a "city" is created using a square surrounded by distinct areas with different functions—cultural, communicative, catering, and functional workspaces. Marcel Wanders designed the Stonehouse with references to a public park and its hedges, rocks and endless deep skies. The majority of the staff at Interpolis prefers to work in this space due to its special, intimate, and subtle outdoor ambiance.

"Who needs a well-lit desk if he can choose to work in the park?"

The contemporary renaissance of humanism

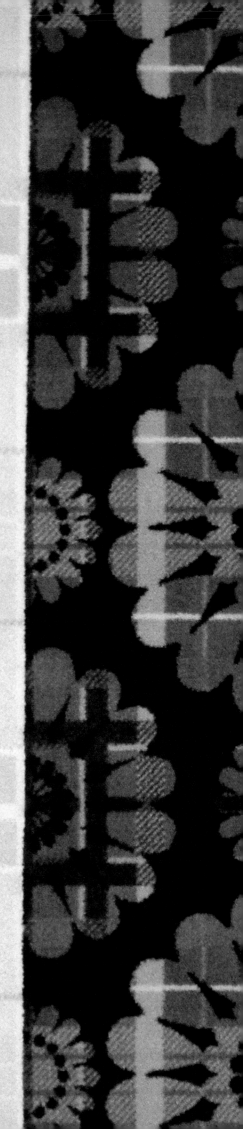

THE CONTEMPORARY RENAISSANCE OF HUMANISM — I remember my early years in design in the early 1980s. As a student I was totally enthusiastic and ready to change the world! To me, design was a deep and refined cultural medium, able to touch humanity in a subtle and caring way and guide it to new and unprecedented heights. I was on a quest to find all the philosophies and ideas—large and small—to support my growing knowledge and dreams.

Reacting to my endless enthusiasm, my teachers and other design heroes used to give me a "more realistic" view, telling me, "Marcel, it's terrible, the people in the street are ignorant, stupid and traditional. They're not interested in the great futuristic designs we try to realize. They have no sense of taste and are unwilling to follow us." I was shocked and couldn't understand why we, being the heros of the future, were so incredibly misunderstood and alone.

Later, I started understanding that in fact our point of view was outdated. Our works were conceptually and visually based on a design theory and sense of style that was created for the first years of the industrial revolution and the early days of industrial design. Architects and designers strived to produce products that could be made by machines and would help create welfare, equality and a political foundation for democracy. They created works that celebrated the limited possibilities of the available machinery. In this period, bending metal tubes and cutting wood with a machine were considered small miracles. Designers created products that were easy to manufacture, but difficult to communicate to an audience who were used to beautiful, crafted, ornamented objects.

Unfortunately, this once interesting quest became a stylistic dogma that still controls works of design today. The industry is far more capable of creating elaborate, fantastic products, but we still follow the traditional dogma and don't use the industry's full potential. We still feel the need to make things easy, economic, functional and simple, instead of inspiring and brilliant—like the qualities of a gift you get from your lover. When I finished school I started understanding that the public perhaps was not as interested in our well-engineered works because they weren't meaningful enough to them. People were looking for more inspirational media. They were not interested in our ancient (design) philosophy and instead wanted more out of life. If I look into the hearts of people, sometimes I can sense what they dream of. If I talk to them I can understand their needs: their need for surprise, for security, for contribution and growth, for individuality and familiarity. Humanity creates an endless flow of illusions and hope.

So many girls want to be beautiful princesses or flying elves; so many boys want to feel like cunning knights or wise kings. Why don't we make it our goal to realize those dreams, and in the meantime, contribute deeply to the lives of others and ourselves? We are allowed to speak the universal language of design that can inspire so many—if we find the right words to speak.

It is our responsibility to be magicians, to be jesters, to be alchemists, to create hope where there is only illusion, to create reality where there are only dreams.

We cannot work for the company who pays us; we have to work for our public and create great value for them. We can no longer use humanity to serve technology; we have to use technology to serve humanity.

Marcel Wanders

BOUTIQUE HOTEL AND CONFERENCE SPACES – 2010

"NOT ANOTHER MINIMALIST DESIGN HOTEL"

Why not break away from the classical dogmas of hospitality design to create a unique hotel and event space where boring corporate events and conferences can be exciting, stimulating and inspiring? The Kameha Grand Bonn has become a place full of surprises, beauty and energy—a place that is sexy and cool. The design itself is exceptional. In order to create intimacy in a building that is dominated by large spaces and extreme transparency, unique solutions had to be found. In the end, the hotel and event area was segmented into small, intimate areas that can be enlarged at any time. Using light, curtains, temporary walls, and textile-covered mobile chandeliers, private "meeting islands" were created in the midst of the vibrant life of the hotel. The ecological lifestyle and design hotel offers first-rate service and high-tech solutions in functionality, while the spa offers a panoramic view onto the Rhine from the outdoor pool on the rooftop terrace. From the Brasserie Next Level to Yu Sushi Club up to the four varied bars and lounges like the Cigar Lounge and the Riverside Terrace, creative food and drink concoctions enchant your plate and mind. Individual suites have various designs. Besides the VIP Royal Suites there are "workaholic rooms," the Ladies Suite, kids rooms, the Fair Play Suite and the Beethoven suite, perfect for those who can't get enough of the full moon above their bed and want to fall asleep listening to Beethoven's whispering Moonlight Sonata.

The Kameha Grand Bonn received the most important award of the German hotel industry when it was rewarded the Hotel of the Year 2011 Award by the Schlummer Atlas editors of the Busche Verlagsgesellschaft. The Kameha Grand Bonn is also winner of the MIPIM Awards 2010 in the Hotels category. The MIPIM Awards recognize excellence and innovation in real estate.

KAMEHA
UNIVERSAL

"Not another minimalist design hotel"

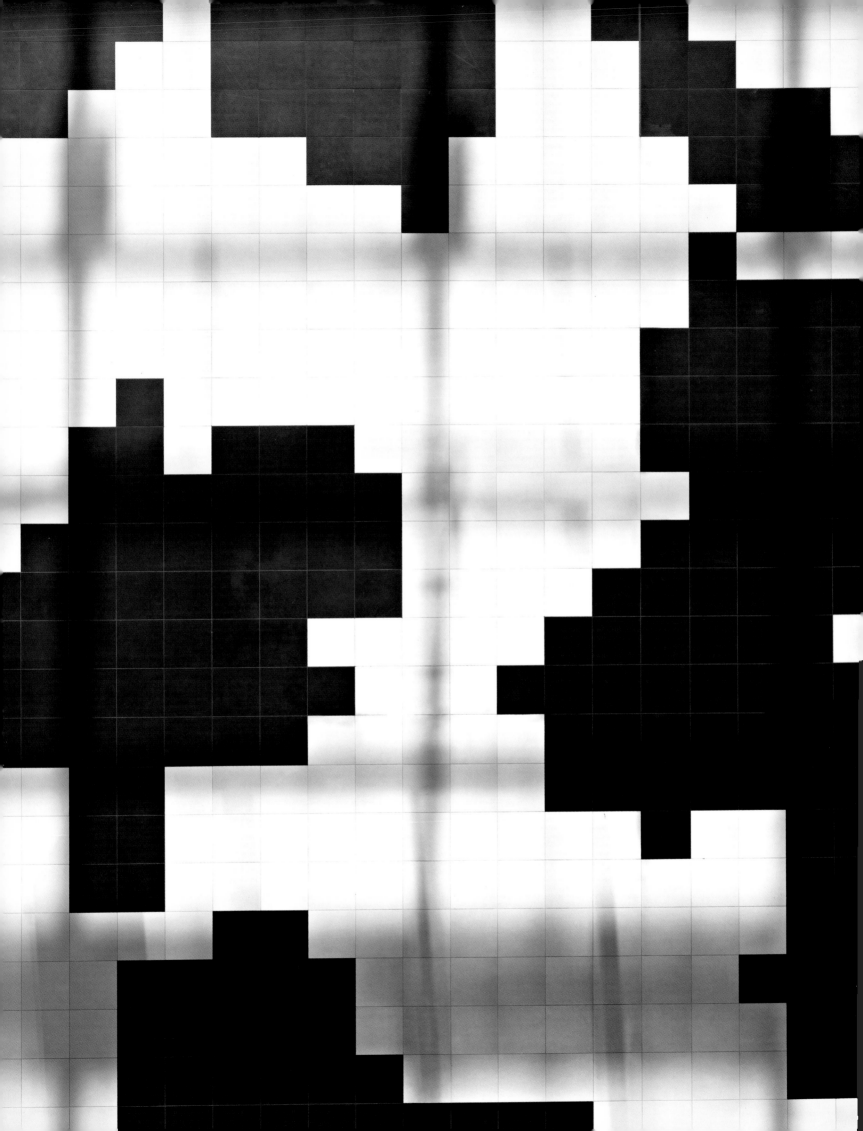

CHAIRMAN'S LOUNGE
BARON PHILIPPE DE
ROTHSCHILD LOUNGE

KING SUITE

Marcel Wanders
Westerstraat 187
1015 MA Amsterdam
tel. +31 (0)204221339
e-mail joy@marcelwanders.com
www.marcelwanders.com

For Marcel Wanders:
Concept and art direction: Marcel Wanders
Book and cover design: Ruben de la Rive Box, Bas Schipper, Roel-Jan Elsinga
Project realization: Annelie Bol, Eva James, Zeynep Musoglu, Earl Singh

Marcel Wanders would like to thank Linda Tischler and Robert Thiemann

A special thanks to the interior team:
Karin Krautgartner, Gerard Fernandez, Kjoep Hommels, Julia Häusser, Marielle Leenen, Jana Kleine-Kalmer, Jana Iszatt, Suzanne Hanson, Robbyn Carter, Douglas van der Pas, Henk van Schuppen, Niels de Jong, Quinten Lans, Anna Langer, Aino Kavantera, Roos Meder, Graham van der Pas, Widya Quasalmy, Rebecca Wijsbeek, Meirav Shitrit, Paulina Deptula, Kristina Geric, Hahna Busch, Marie Guerin, Courtney Clarke, Seon Young Kim, Per Krogsgaard, Monique Engelund Nielsen, Graham Mc Loughlin, Jee Hyun-Min, Frederique Hesp, Marente van der Valk, Timo Nau, Christian Rösner, Lycke von Schantz, Shannon South, Tanny Wong, Rósa Björk, Christina Boskamp, Johannes Diem, Anna Leckström, Anna Ritter, Rodrigo Mendoza, Thomas Baas, Daniel Klapsing, Becky Brisco

First published in the United States of America
by Rizzoli International Publications, Inc.
300 Park Avenue South, New York, NY 10010
www.rizzoliusa.com

Introduction © 2011 Linda Tischler and Robert Thiemann
For Rizzoli International Publications:
Editors: Ian Luna & Lauren A. Gould
Production: Kaija Markoe and Maria Pia Gramaglia
Editorial Assistant: Mandy DeLucia and Kayleigh Jankowski

Rizzoli International Publications would like to thank Eva James, Bas Schipper, Sara Sky Schutte, Goska Sobkowiak, Femke de Wild

Printed in China

2010 2011 2012 2013 / 10 9 8 7 6 5 4 3 2 1
Library of Congress Control Number: 2010938198
ISBN: 978-0-8478-3187-6

Photography credits

Marc Alt – **MONDRIAN SOUTH BEACH** pages 63 and 65 | Tim Bell – **HOTEL ON RIVINGTON** page 76 | Rick Burger for Marcel Wanders – **NOSÉ PORTRAIT** page 2 | Hilde de Decker – **LUTE SUITES** page 101 | Alberto Ferrero – **LUTE SUITES** page 97, page 105, page 111, page 114 | Laurie Lambrecht – **HOTEL ON RIVINGTON** pages 84-85 | copyright Lifestyle Hospitality & Entertainment Group – **KAMEHA GRAND BONN** page 237 above, page 239, pages 245-246 | Marielle van Leenen for Marcel Wanders – **KAMEHA GRAND BONN** page 251 | André Lichtenberg – **MANDARINA DUCK** pages 160-167 | copyright Marcel Wanders – **INTERPOLIS** pages 219-225 | copyright Morgans Hotel Group – **MONDRIAN SOUTH BEACH** pages 56-62, page 64 and pages 66-70, | Nicole Marnati for Marcel Wanders – **CASA SON VIDA** pages 12-27, **VILLA AMSTERDAM** pages 31-51, **VILLA MODA** pages 133-155, **WESTERHUIS** pages 197-215, **KAMEHA GRAND BONN** pages 230-232, pages 234-236, page 237 bottom, pages 240-241, pages 243-244, page 247, page 249-250, page 253 | Jeroen Musch – **BLITS** pages 182-185 | Daniel Nicolas – **EXPO 2000** pages 169-171 | Inga Powilleit, styling by Tatjana Quax – **HOTEL ON RIVINGTON** pages 77-83, **LUTE SUITES** pages 106-110, pages 112-113, page 116-117, **BLITS** 175-181, page 187 bottom | George Terberg – **LUTE SUITES** page 99, page 104 | Nicolas Tosi for ELLE Déco/Scoop – **MONDRIAN SOUTH BEACH** page 71 | Sebastiaan Westerweel – **LUTE SUITES** page 100 | Jonas de Witte – **BLITS** page 175, page 186, page 187 above | Flore Zoé – **LUTE SUITES** page 103, page 115, pages 118-119

Thank you!

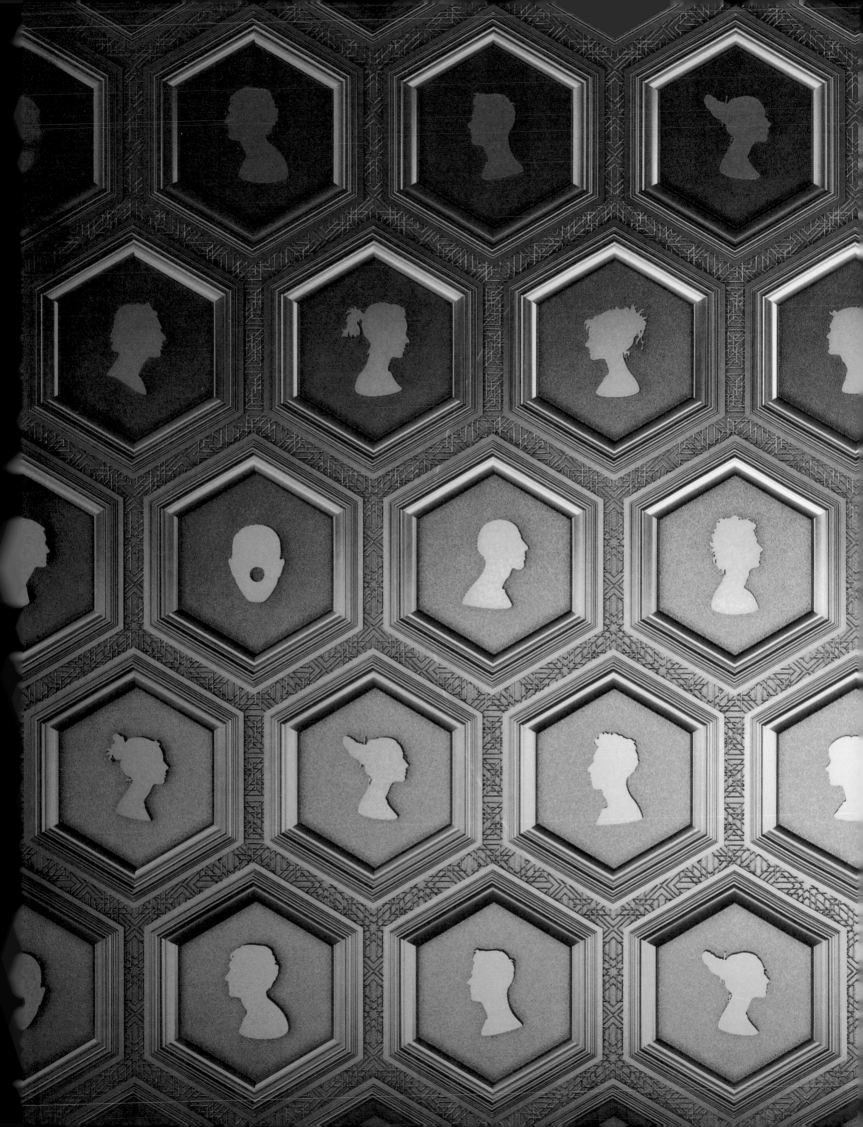